MICHAEL POLLARD

GW00771043

Discoverii
English Folksong

SHIRE PUBLICATIONS LTD

Contents

ACKNOWLEDGEMENTS
    My thanks are due to many friends in the folksong world for their help
and advice, and especially to Topic Records Ltd; and to Mrs Emily Rut-
terford for her help in solving a mystery about *Dives and Lazarus*.
    The cover illustration, *Fanny blooming fair*, is reproduced by kind
permission of Mrs S.G. Allen.

1. The singing English

Folksongs are the songs of the people, handed down from generation to generation by word of mouth. Some of them have a history going back hundreds of years – in some cases so far that their origins have been lost for ever. Others are more recent, either adapted versions of older songs or songs which were completely new in their day and have survived because they were so well liked. It is difficult to lay down firm rules about what is and what is not a folksong, but most people seem to agree that, to qualify, a song must, even if it did once exist in printed form, have spent part of its life out of print and in the mouths of singers. If people learn a song from sheet music or from a recording, they usually sing it exactly as they have learned it, without altering the words or the tune. But if they 'pick it up' from another singer or try to remember it some time – perhaps even some years – after they have heard it sung, they tend to make subtle, unconscious 'improvements' of their own. It is the subtle alterations that take place when songs pass from mouth to mouth – in oral transmission, to use the folksong term – that give folksong much of its interest. Over a long period, a song can alter so much that it becomes a different song; one singer may tack on a happy ending, another may prefer to end on a sad note, another may try the words to a different tune, yet another may simply not be able to manage the tune as he heard it, and so on.

The definition of a folksong as one that has been out of print and in the mouths of singers is a rough and ready one. Probably no two folksong enthusiasts would agree on a precise definition. It is easier, at least for the purposes of this book, to say what is *not* a folksong. Modern songs written in the folk style are not true folksongs. Nor are the tame, cleaned-up and harmonised versions of true folksongs that most of us were taught at school and that can sometimes be heard sung by baritones with piano accompaniment. This book is about true folksongs – what they are, how they were made, who sang them, where they were found and where they can be heard today.

Where did folksongs come from? The answer is: everywhere. Some can be traced back to the great romantic ballads that were sung in the castles and halls of the middle ages. Others tell the kind of story that has always been popular, about faithful (or faithless) lovers, abandoned sweethearts, soldiers marching to war, or brisk and amorous sailors. Yet another large group is of disaster songs, with subjects ranging from the Great Fire of London in 1666 to shipwrecks and pit explosions still within living memory. Then there were the songs about real people, famous or infamous – generals, pirates, highwaymen, sportsmen. Ordinary people, too, have their place, in songs about what it was like to be a child miner or a Greenland whale fisher or a farm labourer on eightpence a day.

England has always been rich in folksong, and songs have been exported for centuries. In Australia and New Zealand, the United States, Canada and wherever English is spoken the songs live on, having been taken there originally by English migrants and settlers. This 'overseas trade' often proves of great value to the folksong collector, who can make use of it to trace songs that have passed out of oral memory in England but which still survive, sometimes disguised and almost unrecognisable, abroad. So in discovering English folksong one finds out a good deal about the folksong of other countries.

The great ballads

In the middle ages one of the few entertainments available was to listen to ballads — stories in song — sung by travelling or, in the houses of the great, resident minstrels. These ballads told long and often complicated stories of heroism and chivalry, sometimes based on real life but usually fictional. The evening meal over, the lords and ladies would settle down to listen to the minstrels. And after the servants had fed from their masters' leavings they would creep in to the back of the hall and on to the balconies to listen to the stories. Some would learn them, or at least parts of them; and so, in time, ballads became an entertainment for the poor as well as the rich. Ballad singers — some good, others very bad — would set up their stalls at fairs and markets. Poor people did not necessarily want to hear about the derring-do of noble knights and their ladies, so many ballads gradually lost their upper-class cast of characters, while still retaining the original story lines.

In this way one ballad could be the starting point for countless folksong versions, with the result that collectors have been able to identify whole families of songs with a common source. One such family is derived from a ballad called *Hynd Horn*, which began life as a story told in the medieval court. *Hynd Horn* variants appear in folksong collections under such titles as *The broken token*, *A fair maid walking in her garden*, *The faithful sailor*, *The dark-eyed sailor* and *Claudy Banks*, among many others. Although all these versions vary to some extent in words and details, all have the same basic *Hynd Horn* plot. A girl out for a walk by the seashore meets a sailor, who asks why she is so sad. She explains that some years before (the number of years varies) she was in love with a sailor, and when he went away to sea they split a gold ring (or sometimes a coin) between them as a keepsake. She has not heard from him since. The sailor then shows the girl his half of the ring, and so the lovers are reunited. (Readers of H.G. Wells's *Kipps* will recognise this as the source of the incident

4

early in the novel when Kipps and his childhood sweetheart Ann split a sixpence between them, and the fact that Wells could use this device in 1905 perhaps shows what a powerful hold the 'broken token' image has on the popular imagination.)

Perhaps, at first sight, it is not remarkable that several songs should have been made on the same theme. Indeed, modern pop songs use and reuse the same ideas over and over again, and romantic fiction has a limited number of plots. What makes the history of *Hynd Horn* unusual (together with that of a number of other great ballads that have come down to us as folksongs) is that not only the story line but some of the details have been preserved intact. In 1898 Mrs Kate Lee, later to be one of the founders of the English Folk Song Society, was noting down songs at Rottingdean in East Sussex, and among the pieces she collected was one called *Claudy Banks*. The heroes of this song were called Betsy and Johnny. A few years later, at a Somerset cottage, the collector Cecil Sharp took down a song which he called *The banks of Claudy* from a Mrs Slade. In 1906 another collector, George Gardiner, listened to a Mr George Blake from Southampton singing a song that he called *The broken token*. The names kept changing; Betsy became Betty, Johnny became William, then Betty became Nancy. But the story remained the same, and so did individual lines of the texts. It is remarkable that Mr James Copper of Rottingdean, Mrs Slade in Somerset, Mr Blake in Southampton and a host of other singers from whom *Hynd Horn* variants were collected round about the same time were singing something that could be traced directly back to the middle ages. How could it happen? Part, at least, of the answer lies in the story of the broadsides.

The broadsides

Although some ballads were written down by early collectors, most of them were passed on by word of mouth. No one knows how many may have disappeared without trace as their singers died. But the invention of printing changed all that. For about three hundred years, from the middle of the sixteenth century to the middle of the nineteenth (and lingering on up to, and beyond, the First World War), broadsides enabled folksongs to be learned and passed on. They were crudely printed song-sheets, containing words only and printed on just one side of the paper, which were sold on the streets and at fairs and markets. There were no popular newspapers or magazines in those days, and so broadsides were almost the only reading matter available to ordinary people, and they were also the only source of news. People in those days did not have the thirst for news that we have today; since few of them had the vote, they had no need to keep abreast of politics, for example. But they liked to hear of victories against the French, of notable murders (especially if the details were grisly) and of personalities in the news. Sold all over England by the thousand (and some of the most popular ones are said to have sold more than a million), broadsides were the nearest most people ever got to news. And broadside printers were the forerunners of today's press barons, though without their political power.

Some broadsides were based on the old ballads, but most dealt with current or recent events: the execution of Captain Kidd in 1701, General Wolfe's death at the Battle of Abraham Heights in 1759, Trafalgar in 1805, the murder of Maria Marten in 1827, and so on. Ballad-mongers sold their broadsides by singing them, so that the buyer had a chance to learn the tune before he bought the words. No doubt many of the ballad-mongers were poor singers, so that oral transmission was unreliable; and no doubt some of the customers, later repeating what they had heard, introduced accidental or deliberate variations in tune or words or both, or even decided to adapt the words to a tune they liked more.

Tunes are generally less easy to come by than words, and certain tunes did service time after time. An example is the *Admiral Benbow* air, as it is usually known although it was in use before Benbow's time. It was used for a broadside sold at the public execution of the pirate Captain Kidd at Execution Dock in London in 1701, and for one produced for another public hanging, of a chimney-sweep named Jack Hall, in the same year. (Hall's offence, by comparison with Kidd's, was trivial; it was burglary.) In 1702 Benbow defeated the French fleet after a four-day battle in the Caribbean, and the tune was used again for a broadside about the victory. In Queen Victoria's time it was still being used as a setting for songs about criminals, the name and details of the crime being changed appropriately to cover the case of a felon currently in the news.

So what effect would the broadside printers have on the progress of the great ballads like *Hynd Horn*? There was no copyright law in those days, and there was nothing to prevent a printer in, say, Birmingham resetting a broadside he had bought in London, putting his own name at the bottom, and selling it as his own production, and this is often what happened. The printing of broadsides was a useful sideline for many provincial jobbing printers, keeping their workforce and machines occupied if there was nothing more urgent to do. But some printers may have wanted to introduce a few embellishments of their own, or to change a few names and details so that their broadside was recognisably theirs. That was how Johnny became William, and Betty became Nancy. In some versions of *Hynd Horn* the faithful girl finds on the seashore not her long-lost lover but his body, and in searching for means of identification comes across the broken token. So it was that the broadsides picked up the old stories, put a gloss on them, sometimes cheapened them, but kept them alive.

One of the leading broadside printers was James Catnach, who established his business in Seven Dials, London, in 1814. He set out to corner the market, and for him the production of broadsides was the bulk of his business. He bought material from ballad-mongers who came to see him and at one time kept a fiddler on hand to check that the words would fit to well known tunes. The Catnach business lasted for almost a century, and one of its achievements (even though the proprietor was interested only in the money) was to rescue innumerable folksong versions of ballads, including *Hynd Horn*. His version, published in the 1830s as *Phoebe and her dark-eyed sailor* (yet another change of name for the girl), is said by the folklorist A. L. Lloyd to be the source of all the variants collected around 1900. However, this seems unlikely, and unfair to the resourcefulness of Victorian broadside entrepreneurs. Although, through all its variations, the *Hynd Horn* story remains recognisable, there have clearly been other hands at work, and these were probably pirate printers working by candlelight in Bristol, Nottingham and elsewhere. The *Hynd Horn* story was what would today be called a 'standard'. Against the lack of a good murder or a bloody battle, it was no doubt worth having a few songs like *Hynd Horn* available.

The growth of the popular press in the later nineteenth century gradually killed the broadside business, though as late as 1940 there was at least one ballad-monger still at work in central London. Meanwhile, many of the broadside songs passed into memory and went on being sung and learned by new singers. This continued circulation of the songs was helped by the fact that many buyers of broadsides pasted them on their walls at home, where they might last a generation or so before becoming indecipherable.

However, of the many thousands of broadsides printed relatively few have come down to us as folksongs. Many, especially the more topical ones, had a very short life and failed to catch on. Copies can still be seen in local library and museum collections, but the majority are probably not worth rescuing and putting back into circulation. In any case, if they had no real life in oral tradition they can hardly qualify as folksongs.

Folk plays and calling-on songs

One of the features of fairs and popular festivals from the thirteenth century onwards was the performance of simple plays by groups of travelling players. They would set up a stall or use the back of a wagon as a stage and act out stories from the Bible or the Apocrypha. The Nativity story was popular, but the Apocrypha were the source of the best known and most widely acted of these plays, *St George and the Dragon*.

There were no scripts. The actors learned their parts by watching other actors and often took liberties with their material, introducing new characters or incidents into the stories. Like pantomime actors today, they would add local allusions or bring in local worthies. Father Christmas, the Turkish Knight, comic doctors or constables and even real-life heroes like Nelson might also be brought in.

The cast was usually introduced before the play began with a 'calling-on song' in which each character would step forward and sing a verse about himself. The song would often be heard again at the end, with a last verse asking the audience to be generous when the hat was passed round.

The song *We wish you a merry Christmas* is the last surviving fragment of one of these songs, with the actors asking at the end not for money but for refreshments. The songs that accompany the May Day ceremonies at Padstow, Helston and other towns in Cornwall and Devon are further examples, while in Yorkshire and Lancashire there are surviving calling-on songs associated with Easter plays.

Industrial songs

From about 1800 England became increasingly a nation earning its living from industry rather than the land. This had two effects on folksong.

First, people who moved to the towns and cities often looked back longingly (though not always with good reason) to the 'old days' in the country, and so songs with rural themes, about girls going nutting and swains stepping out across the dewy fields on a fine May morning, took on a new lease of life. But at the same time, some songs were adapted to reflect the new way of life in the city. *Jim the carter lad* became *Jack the factory lad*, *The rambling ploughboy* became *The rambling miner*, and so on.

It was not long before the industrial towns and cities began to have folksongs of their own. There was plenty of material: the contrast between the life styles of millowners and their employees, the horrors of child labour, the decline of hand weaving, and so on. Some were printed as broadsides and – later in the nineteenth century – some appeared in local newspapers, but many had no life in print and were passed on in the old country style.

One of the latter sort was *Poverty knock*, a lament for the life of a factory weaver: work starts at five o'clock and there are fines for latecomers; the work is backbreaking and dangerous; the looms are not maintained properly and the threads keep breaking; and throughout the song runs the refrain of 'poverty, poverty knock', said to mimic the sound of the loom. Though now in the repertoire of many folk club singers, *Poverty knock* seems to have been collected only once in only one version. In 1965 it was taken down from the singing of an old Batley weaver who had first heard it being sung in the mill some sixty years earlier. No broadside from which the song might have come has ever been discovered, and the detail in the text suggests that it was produced by a weaver, not a printer's hack. In many ways it is a typical industrial song, but it is curious that its tune is based on the German lullaby *Schlaf, mein Prinzchen, schlaf ein*. How this came to be in the repertoire of a weaver in Batley is one of the mysteries of folksong.

Music hall, chapel and club

Living in towns and cities, people had more opportunities than they had had before to get together and sing. Working hours were long, but when the working day was finally over there was little inducement to stay at home in the mean back-to-back houses built for the masses. The brewing industry prospered because of the workers' need for somewhere warm and light to spend their leisure hours – and so did the music hall.

In its early days the music hall relied heavily on folksongs and their tunes, and many early performers made a speciality of folksong parodies – some of which have lasted better than the originals. On Tyneside, for example, the comedian Joe Wilson (who wrote *Keep your feet still, Geordie Hinny*, among many other songs) took *Pretty little Polly Perkins*, a rather sickly-sweet Cockney parody of an earlier song, and turned it into *Cushie Butterfield*, an altogether more earthy girl. In London, the Cockney comedian Sam Cowell produced several parodies which went on to live in folk memory in their own right. Among them was *Villikins and Dinah (Toorali oorali oorali ay)*. This had started life as a broadside based on the murder of Maria Marten in 1827, *William and Maria*, which, Stephen Sedley has written, 'was so awful in itself that the text barely had to be changed to achieve a handsome send-up'. But *Villikins and Dinah* went on to live its own broadside life, and it is in this form that the song is known today. Cowell gave similar treatment to the old and respectable ballad *The banks of green willow*, about a sailor who drowns his pregnant girl friend. In this case, the original lived on to be recovered by later collectors, but Cowell's brisker and less tender version also survived into the twentieth century.

Music halls were not the only meeting places for the industrial population. Just as significant were the nonconformist chapels which sprang up in every community – sometimes in rivalry next door to each other – and, in their struggle for popular support, often set hymns to familiar folksong tunes. With their Services of Song, Pleasant Sunday Afternoons, Women's Joyful Hours, Sunday School Anniversary Meetings, Pleasant Saturday Nights and other regular events, the chapels were true community centres and provided many opportunities for secular as well as sacred singing. On a Pleasant Saturday Night, the contributions would often include a song drawn from a ballad or broadside, usually with a suitably moral last verse tacked on, set to a folk tune. Sometimes, tunes did not adapt easily to hymns; generations of Baptist chapelgoers were required to sing, to a variant of the folk tune *Dives and Lazarus*, 'Stir up my stu, stir up my stu, stir up my stupid soul'.

A further influence on folksong was the working-class movement. When people were working in larger groups and living in larger communities they became more conscious of the events shaping their lives, and the political movements of the nineteenth century produced songs which again leaned upon folksong as a source of tunes. Some early trade unions had their own songbooks, though few unionised folksongs have survived in oral tradition.

Disaster songs

During the nineteenth century a large number of terrible civil disasters occurred — hundreds of miners lost in one explosion, hundreds of immigrants drowned in a single shipwreck, naval ships lost with all hands. Such disasters were taken as themes for songs, sometimes simply for their news value and sometimes, especially in mining areas, to raise money for the victims' families. In the pits, the tradition of fund-raising disaster songs persisted until at least 1934. In that year, an explosion at Gresford Colliery near Wrexham in North Wales killed over 260 men, and the bitter anti-coalowners song that resulted is still to be heard in folk clubs.

Travelling songs

Emigrants take their culture with them to remind them of home, and this was as true of British settlers in America and Australia as it was of the post-war West Indians who went to Britain. Especially in the more remote parts of the new homelands like the Kentucky Mountains in America and the Australian outback, English folksongs lived on, sometimes word for word and note for note as they had been sung back home, and sometimes taking on the colouring of the new way of life. Many of them were to return home later. Reworked versions of the old songs were discovered in the 1920s by pioneer sound recordists and crossed the Atlantic once again as hillbilly, country and bluegrass numbers.

The music

Much of what has been written so far concerns the words of folksongs. But what about the tunes? There are fewer folksong tunes than there are sets of words, the tunes having been used and reused with minor variations or with none at all. *Villikins and Dinah*, for example, must have been sung to hundreds of different sets of words. As anyone who has tried knows, it is easier to write new words to an existing tune than to start from nothing.

English folksong was originally sung unaccompanied, the singer providing some 'trimmings' himself by way of grace notes and vibratos. There was no harmonisation and no strict time, and a bar might be extended indefinitely if this was necessary to accommodate the words. Purist lovers of folksong still prefer to hear it sung that way, and there are still some performers who sing in the old style. But for most people the songs are more accessible if they are accompanied and arranged to conform with modern musical conventions. This can easily be taken too far, as with the piano arrangements for schools mentioned earlier and with heavily instrumental arrangements for folksy pop groups; but some ordering of the music, with guitar or perhaps concertina accompaniment in a fairly unobtrusive style, provides a compromise which does not destroy the intrinsic quality of the music but enables more people to enjoy it. In the folksong world, old-style singing is spoken of as 'the tradition' and the newer style as 'the revival'.

Much scholarship has been devoted to the analysis of folk music, but this book will not deal with such hotly argued issues as tonality, modes and the relationship between the folk and classical conventions of music. For discussion of these matters, with copious musical examples, the reader is referred to chapters 5-7 of Cecil Sharp's *English Folk Song: Some Conclusions* (fourth edition, revised and edited by Maud Karpeles, Mercury Books, 1965) – though some of Sharp's views have been disputed – or A. L. Lloyd's *Folk Song in England* (Lawrence and Wishart, 1967/Paladin, 1975).

How English is English folksong?

Although it is common to hear items introduced as 'an old West Country song' or 'a song they sing up in Yorkshire', it is dangerous to be too dogmatic about where a folksong actually comes from. Ballad singers and broadside sellers often covered large areas of England, and many songs were passed on by wagoners, drovers, packmen, travelling pedlars and others who spent most of their working lives on the road. Soldiers and sailors, too, were active 'carriers' of folksong. The result is that a song may be 'from the West Country' only in the sense that it was heard by a collector in one of the western counties.

The same is true of many songs commonly thought of as Scottish, Welsh or Irish. Songs in the Gaelic, Welsh and Irish languages and their music have tended to keep their separate identity, but songs in English have travelled freely, while English songs have taken on a new life of their own in other parts of Britain. This is not surprising when one considers the large movements of population that have taken place since the beginning of the nineteenth century. With the exception of relatively few songs that are distinctive of their region and peculiar to it, versions of English folksongs — sometimes suitably adapted with different placenames or characters — are likely to be found in any part of the British Isles.

Nevertheless, songs from Scotland, Wales or Ireland tend to take on a kind of Englishness when they settle in England. Names are changed, dialect phrases are altered, and there are subtle variations in tunes. Perhaps the only thing that can safely be said is that any folksong collected from oral tradition in England counts as an English folksong.

2. The discovery of folksong

The early collectors

Folksong collecting began with the invention of printing. No doubt there were singers in earlier times who made collections of songs for their own use, but they would have carried them in their heads. Folksong was too lowly an art to attract the interest of the few people who could read and write. In any case, their rare skills were absorbed in religious works, legal documents and a handful of works of literature.

But in 1476 William Caxton set up England's first printing press, and within twenty years his successor, Wynken de Worde, had published the first English broadsides, a set of ballads based on the Robin Hood stories. From then on, broadsides came off the presses in an ever increasing stream – to the alarm of the government. This flood of popular literature could possibly have become subversive, and some kind of control was necessary. From the middle of the sixteenth century all publishers of broadsides were required to register them at Stationers' Hall and over the next century and a half over three thousand titles were so registered.

At about the same time the first collections were started. The early collectors were antiquarians who were mainly interested in ballads of the older sort and their connection with literature. One of these was a lawyer and member of Parliament, John Selden, whose collection was bought after his death by the diarist Samuel Pepys. By the time Pepys died in 1703 he had amassed some eighteen hundred items, including not only examples of the great classical ballads but also more trivial pieces that he had bought from street vendors. It is due to Pepys, whose collection still exists at Cambridge, that the history of many songs can be traced back so far – and also that we have a record of many ephemeral pieces that would otherwise have disappeared. One example of the latter kind is a broadside account of the Great Fire of London, *London mourning in ashes*. No doubt Pepys bought this in the street; it is clear from his diary that he often took home broadsides and sheet music for the amusement of his family and household.

London mourning in ashes contains a precise description of the outbreak and spread of the fire as detailed as anything that might have been found in the newspapers of the time if they had existed. And it ends, like many ballads and broadsides, on a moral note:

> If this do not reform our lives
> A worse thing shall succeed.
> Our kindred, children, and our wives
> Will die for want of bread.

13

When famine comes, 'tis not our drums,
　　Our ships, our horse and foot
That can defend, but if we mend
　　We never shall come to't.

Another important early collector was Thomas Percy, Bishop of Dromore in Ireland. In 1765 he published his collection of almost two hundred ballads, *Reliques of Ancient English Poetry* ('consisting', said the title page, 'of old heroic ballads, songs, and other pieces of our earlier poets, together with some few of later date'). He took his ballads from the Pepys collection and from other sources, but he does not seem to have been interested in the broadsides of his own time. As a result, the collection is something of a museum piece. He also fell to the temptation that afflicted many later collectors: the desire to 'improve' the original ballads according to the literary criteria of the time and partly to 'admit nothing immoral or indecent'. The collection is therefore not as interesting as it might have been, though it is still useful in tracing the sources of the older ballads.

As the broadsides increased their circulations, appealing mainly to the working class, collectors lost interest in them. At the same time, literary interest in the past turned, in the later eighteenth century, towards ancient Greece and Rome. There was a gap of about a century between Percy and the next group of serious collectors.

The nineteenth century

This next group was not of antiquarians pursuing a gentle hobby, but of publishers concerned with producing profitable books. The best known and most comprehensive of these books was *Popular Music of the Olden Time*, published by William Chappell in 1859, but there were many others, many of them regional. John Bell of Newcastle was early in the field with *Rhymes of the Northern Bards* (1812), followed by John Harland's *Ballads and Songs of Lancashire* and Frank Kidson's *Traditional Tunes* (1891) from Yorkshire. In the last half of the century Francis Child, a Harvard University professor of English, put together his massive collection of *English and Scottish Popular Ballads*, a scholarly undertaking which is still one of the masterworks of folksong study.

However, these were all primarily, if not exclusively, collections that had been made from other printed sources or from memory. The nineteenth-century collectors did not go to the singers and take down their songs direct; this was left to a later generation. Meanwhile, folksong was still living a real life of its own, away from publishers' offices and scholars' studies. For most people, folksong was the only kind of music available, and so it was inevitable that if they sang at all that was what they sang. Many songs were being preserved by the soldiers who marched to them, the sailors who hauled ropes to them and the fisher-girls who gutted herring to them.

Reference was made in the previous chapter to the preservative influence of political and religious movements and of the music hall. One of the familiar tunes to which the hymn *All things bright and beautiful* is sung is the folk tune *The twenty-ninth of May*. The usual tune of Bunyan's hymn *To be a pilgrim* is of folk origin. The Salvation Army took the tune of *O no John* (whose words were hardly suited to religious use) and provided it with a new text entitled *Yes, Lord*. *The red flag* was originally written to fit an English folksong tune, though in the event an alternative was chosen. The song *The roast beef of old England* was used for many years as a party campaign song, originally by the Tories but later, with suitably ironic words, by supporters of the working-class movement. In the early days of the nineteenth century, for example, it was adapted as *The hard times of old England*, a bitter comment on prices, low wages, unemployment and poor living conditions. A similar fate befell another rousing patriotic song, *A fine old English gentleman* ('one of the old brigade'), which inspired a number of merciless parodies including one by Charles Dickens.

Although the political or religious use of folksongs or their tunes was not 'collecting' in the usual sense, it helped to keep them alive in much the same way. Indeed, it added to the repertoire of folksongs, because *The roast beef of old England* and *A fine old English gentleman*, for example, were composed 'gentlemen's' songs until their parodies passed into oral tradition.

The parson collectors

Clergymen in rural parishes in Victorian England often kept notes of traditional customs and ways of life, partly as a mere hobby and partly because they felt that, in an age of change, old memories should be preserved. This led many parsons to an interest in folksong, and one of these was the Reverend William Barnes, rector of Winterborne Came in Dorset.

William Barnes is best known as a writer of poems in the Dorset dialect, of which he published four books widely admired at the time. He came to folksong through his interest in language, and for the last four or five years of his life — he died in 1886 — he contributed an anonymous 'Folklore Column' to the *Dorset County Chronicle* in which he often included folksongs. Some of these he had personally collected from the singers, and he was possibly one of the first parson collectors to work in this way. But folksong was just one of his many interests, and only a sideline leading from his interest in philology; he died before he could develop it any further, and although he noted a few rare songs he cannot be regarded as an important collector. Nonetheless, the way he stumbled across folksong through his interest in folklore generally is typical of how the country clergy began collecting.

About the same time as William Barnes was starting his desultory collecting in Dorset, the Reverend Sabine Baring-Gould became rector of Lew Trenchard in Devon. Like Barnes, Baring-Gould was a man of many parts. In his ninety years – he died in 1924 – he wrote some fifty novels, many in several volumes, an opera, countless religious works, biographies of Nelson and Napoleon among others, about twenty guidebooks, a similar number of general books, pamphlets on subjects ranging from Wagner's *Parsifal* to *How to save fuel*, and – the only one of his works to have lasted – the hymn *Onward, Christian soldiers*. It was a chance remark over the dinner table about the way the old songs were dying out that led him to embark on a programme to rescue them. He told his host how, as a boy, he had ridden round Dartmoor, putting up at small inns, and had heard men singing ballads as they sat and smoked. 'My host said to me,' he wrote later, '"Come, you are the man to undertake the job of collecting these songs and airs. It must be done at once, or it cannot be done at all, for in a few years they will be lost."'

An indefatigable enthusiast, Baring-Gould walked home from the dinner party with, as he said, his mind in a ferment. He started work at once, and in the next two years, from 1888 to 1890, he tracked down over sixty old men and three women singers, for the most part travelling on foot. He could cope with music only at the piano, so he had to sing the tunes over and over to himself until he reached home. Later, he overcame this problem by recruiting two more musically gifted fellow clergymen, and sometimes by inviting the more hale and hearty old men to visit his house, where he plied them with ale in front of the fire and picked out their tunes on the piano as they sang them, repeating them to check that they were right.

In an attempt to make the songs more widely known, Baring-Gould went 'on tour' with his two collecting colleagues, the sister of one of them as accompanist, and occasionally members of his own family, presenting musical evenings in towns all over Devon and Cornwall. But the concert-going middle class took little interest, and he lost heavily on the venture. The publication of his four books of West Country folksongs was, however, more successful. The first, *The Songs of the West*, was published in parts between 1889 and 1891, with a one-volume edition following in 1892. *A Garland of Country Song* followed in 1895, the eight volumes of *English Minstrelsie* between 1895 and 1897, and finally *English Folk Songs for Schools*, on which he collaborated with Cecil Sharp, in 1906. After that, his interest in the subject seems to have waned, and it has been suggested that he resented the limelight that fell upon Sharp as a pioneer collector. However, as he was by now over seventy it may be simply that he could no longer undertake the arduous travelling that his method of collecting had entailed.

It was slow, painstaking work, seeking out the old country singers in pubs and clubs, workhouses and almshouses. Many singers were shy about their songs and reluctant to sing them to strangers, especially to strangers in clerical collars. Often, when what he wanted to hear was genuine folksong, Baring-Gould would be offered a schoolroom memory like *Rule Britannia* or *Hearts of oak*. It was not always possible, even with the help of competent musicians, to arrive at the definitive version of a tune, or even of the words, when sung by an old man with a failing memory and a quavering voice.

Unfortunately Baring-Gould, like many other collectors from Bishop Percy onwards, did alter the words of the songs. A proficient versifier, as his hymnbooks showed, he set himself to 'improve' those ballads which, as he wrote, 'reveal a rudeness of manner and moral that make it impossible for me to publish the words exactly'. But, fortunately, he deposited a copy of his manuscript collection, containing over two hundred songs, with the Plymouth City Library, so that the songs of late Victorian Devon and Cornwall can still be studied as they were taken down from the mouths of singers some of whom were repeating words and tunes they had learned as children not long after Trafalgar, from grandparents who could remember the coronation of George III.

Baring-Gould was the most industrious of the parson collectors, but many others were at work. As early as 1843, the Reverend John Broadwood was collecting in Sussex and on the Surrey border. The diary of the Reverend Francis Kilvert, curate of Clyro in Wales from 1865 to 1872, shows that he collected traditional songs, though apparently fairly spasmodically, and the collection, if it ever reached that degree of formality, has not survived. In Dorset, as well as the Reverend William Barnes, the Reverends Canon Mayo and Herbert Pentin were keen collectors, publishing their finds in *Somerset and Dorset Notes and Queries* and the *Journal of the Dorset Field Club*. But the most important event in the history of modern English folksong collecting was still to come, and it occurred in the house of yet another parson.

Cecil Sharp

In 1903, when he was forty-three, a music lecturer named Cecil Sharp went to stay for a few days with a parson friend, the Reverend Charles Marson, at Hambridge in Somerset. They had a common interest in folk music, but it was on that holiday in 1903 that Sharp noted down his first folksong. It was from his host's gardener, whose name was John England. The song was *The seeds of love*:

> I sowed the seeds of love
>> And I sowed them in the spring.
> I gathered them up in the morning early
>> While the small birds sweetly sing,
>> While the small birds sweetly sing.

The song, sung to a version of the old *Admiral Benbow* air mentioned in the previous chapter, was already known to collectors, and Sharp's version was one of countless variants noted from all over England, including two collected by Baring-Gould. All are apparently descended from a song either written or collected by a gentlewoman in Lancashire in 1689. But to Sharp the song, and in particular the manner in which it was sung, was a new experience. Fired with enthusiasm, he joined the English Folk Song Society, then only five years old, and over the next twenty-one years, until his death in 1924 (the same year as Baring-Gould), he collected nearly five thousand songs in England and North America. (Many of these were variants, however, not completely distinct songs, and by no means all of them were fresh discoveries.)

Cecil Sharp was the most important and industrious collector of English folksongs during his lifetime, before or after, and no critical comment can deny him that distinction. But because he was interested in publishing his finds, sensibly believing that songs could only live on if they were learned and sung, and because he saw schools both commercially as his main market and as the most hopeful agencies of preservation, he was forced to tidy up the tunes to make them acceptable for simple piano arrangement, and, worse, he had to censor the words, which led him in many songs to replace the fresh and simple earthiness of rural sentiments by wishy-washy, prettified images and sometimes by complete nonsense. In this, Baring-Gould collaborated with him.

Sharp himself recognised the dilemma. 'However much we may admire the simplicity and the straightforward diction of the ballad maker,' he wrote in *English Folk Song: Some Conclusions*, published in 1907, 'we have to realise that other times and other people are not so simple-minded and downright, and that what is deemed fit and proper for one period is not necessarily so for others.' The world revealed by folksong was not one that respectable Victorians and Edwardians cared to contemplate. It was a world in which girls too often found that their apron strings would not tie; in which men and women made love with few preliminaries and sometimes even without an introduction; in which 'briskness' (lust) was a heroic virtue and maidenheads were best disposed of as soon as possible as an unnecessary hindrance. Clearly schoolchildren could not be invited to sing of such things, or their teachers to teach them; nor were the songs, as they stood, suitable fare for musical evenings intended to celebrate the virtues of family life. But the result was that many songs which were excellent when taken down from the original singers – *Strawberry fair* and *O no John* are two examples – have become such broken-down hack pieces for piano and unison voices that they are now virtually unsingable, and indeed have, for generations of children forced to sing them, given the whole of folksong a bad name.

Cecil Sharp admitted that he was more interested in the music of folksong than in the words, and consequently he felt less reluctance to alter the words to suit his market. However, it is often possible to reconstruct the original words by comparing Sharp's version with those of other collectors. The serious student may consult Sharp's original notebooks – rude words and all – at Clare College, Cambridge, and in 1958 the poet James Reeves performed a great service to folksong when he published *The Idiom of the People*, containing the texts of about one hundred and twenty songs taken directly from the notebooks.

There are two other criticisms frequently made of Sharp. One is that he defined folksong too narrowly, excluding what he called 'vulgar street songs' and possibly, as a result, allowing to die songs which could, if he had preserved them at least in his notebooks, have found a welcome in succeeding generations. (He gives his own definition of folksong in the first chapter of *English Folk Song: Some Conclusions.)*

Since the argument about what makes a folksong still goes on with no sign of being resolved, it is perhaps unfair to criticise Sharp for at least attempting a definition, especially as he was so early in the field, with little folk music scholarship to guide him.

The other criticism is that, along with other collectors of his time, he tended to publish his songs (no doubt for commercial reasons) as county collections, giving rise to the idea that, say, Somerset has one set of indigenous songs and Dorset another. Although there are exceptions, most folksongs occur widely in various parts of England (to say nothing of overseas), with only slight variations. England is not a large country, and even before the days of railways and asphalt roads a surprising number of people moved about in it, mainly in the course of their work. A wagoner might hear a song in Hampshire and sing it again in Sussex. A drover returning from Norfolk to Yorkshire might bring back with him a whole clutch of new songs, having sung some in Lincolnshire on the way. A song that happened to have been collected in a Hampshire almshouse might equally 'belong' to a dozen counties. There are few folksongs which an individual county or even region can claim as its very own.

The Folk Song Society

The Folk Song Society was founded in 1899, its committee dominated by members of the musical establishment such as Stainer, Stanford and Parry. None of these had ever shown any particular interest in folksong, all being committed to choral and church music, but they were in a position to influence academic thinking and so obtain support for folksong studies. Among the collectors on the committee were Lucy Broadwood, who had carried on the work of her father, the Reverend John Broadwood, in the south-east and had published *English County Songs* in 1893, and Frank Kidson, whose collection of Yorkshire songs, *Traditional Tunes*, had come out in 1891.

There were about a hundred founder members, but Cecil Sharp was not among them. He had, at that time, still to experience his first taste of folk music, which came at Christmas 1899, when he was visiting a friend near Oxford and saw morris dancing for the first time. Baring-Gould was, however, one of the society's first members, and the honour of noting the first folksong on behalf of the society went to Mrs Kate Lee who, at Rottingdean in East Sussex, noted down *Claudy Banks* from the singing of the Copper family.

Sharp joined the society early in 1904, a few months after hearing John England sing *The seeds of love*, and at once began to attack its members for their apathy. (There was perhaps an echo of an earlier quarrel here, for a few years before Sharp had clashed with Parry in an academic wrangle whose correspondence Sharp had published.) Perhaps the society's members enjoyed his combative spirit, because within a year he had been elected to the committee and had taken over a whole issue of the society's annual *Journal*. His collaboration with Baring-Gould, which was to result in *Songs of the West* (1905) and *English Folk Songs for Schools* (1906), had already begun, and Sharp, working fast, must already have started thinking about *English Folk Song: Some Conclusions*, which he published in 1907.

Sharp's enthusiasm stimulated others into action. Two of these were retired classics teachers, Henry Hammond and George Gardiner, who co-operated in collecting their first songs in 1905 but later went their separate ways. Hammond, with his brother Robert, embarked on a series of cycling tours in Dorset primarily, but also in Somerset, Worcestershire and Wiltshire. In three years' work they collected some six hundred songs. Gardiner also took up folksong as a retirement hobby, working mainly in Hampshire but also in Wiltshire, Surrey and Sussex. His achievement, now strangely neglected, was some fifteen hundred songs and variants which, though deposited with the society, have not yet been fully explored. Both Hammond and Gardiner died in 1910.

But the major figure in the early days of the English Folk Song

Society, surpassing Sharp himself in musical stature, was Vaughan Williams. He collected his first song – it was *Bushes and briars* – in Essex in December 1903 and over the next ten years noted hundreds of tunes but very much fewer sets of words. This extensive exposure to folk tunes soon began to be reflected in his compositions such as the *Norfolk Rhapsodies, On Wenlock Edge* and the overture to *The Wasps*. The influence of folksong remained in his later, major compositions, and it spread, too, into his musical editorship of *The English Hymnal* and *The Oxford Book of Carols*, both of which he enriched with folk tune settings. His interest in folksong remained throughout his life, and when Penguin Books proposed to bring out a book of English folksongs he was a natural choice as joint editor with A. L. Lloyd. Sadly, he had died by the time the book appeared in 1959. Vaughan Williams was president of the Folk Song Society in 1930, when the first moves were made towards amalgamating it with the English Folk Dance Society, with which it had so much (including many members, among them Vaughan Williams himself) in common. He is generally thought to have been the main architect of the link, which was formalised in 1932 to the great benefit of all with an interest in folk music.

Another important collector of the time was Percy Grainger. Not only did he use folk tunes in his own work and compose arrangements of such folk pieces as *Country gardens*, but also he was the first collector in Britain to record folksongs mechanically. He conducted two extensive recording sessions in Lincolnshire in 1906 and 1908, and it is said that the majority of his wax cylinders from those occasions remain untranscribed. Grainger, who was Australian, emigrated to the United States in 1915, taking his collection with him, and it is now housed in the Percy Grainger Library at White Plains, New York.

With the invention of the recording machine – though a very primitive one at that stage – and the interruption to folksong collecting by the First World War, the golden age of collecting in England can be said to have ended. It had been a remarkable ten years or so, and during it most of what is known today about English folksong was discovered.

3. The singers

By all accounts, the singers were grand old men and women. There were Moses Cleave of Huckaby Bridge, Dartmoor, Jonas Crocker of Belstone, Roger and William Huggins, masons, of Lydford, Suey Stevens, a charwoman, of Stowford, and Sally Satterley of Huckaby Bridge, to quote a few names at random from Baring-Gould's list of singers. We cannot, however, know what they thought of the parsons, musical academics and retired classics masters who advanced upon them, notebook and pencil in hand. The collectors seem for the most part to have felt well satisfied with their contacts, and Baring-Gould and Sharp in particular reported in some detail on the personalities of the singers.

The early collectors were embarking on what they clearly felt to be an adventure. Though a Fabian (and also, paradoxically, a member of the Navy League), Sharp had spent all his working life, apart from two years at the beginning when he was reading law, teaching music, and he cannot have had much contact with the working classes. Baring-Gould's contacts would have been as squire and parson. But there was a pioneering spirit abroad and in his introduction to Sharp's first songbook, *Folk Songs from Somerset*, in 1904, his friend the Reverend Charles Marson wrote (before the schools discovered folksong): 'Folksong, unknown in the drawing-room, hunted out of the school, chased by the chapel deacons, derided by the middle classes, and despised by those who have been uneducated into the three Rs, takes refuge in the fastnesses of tap-rooms, poor cottages and outlying hamlets.' One of Baring-Gould's singers, seventy-six year old Roger Luxton of Halwill, North Devon, put it more pithily: 'The farmers be too grand to talk to us chaps, and for certain they don't care to hear us zing. Why, for nigh on forty years us old zingin-fellows have been drove to the public houses to zing.'

To their enthusiasm the collectors added desperation. Time was running out, they were convinced, and a sense of urgency runs through much of what they wrote about their work. 'We cannot shut our eyes', wrote a Dorset collector, the Reverend Herbert Pentin, in 1906, 'to the fact that the old traditional songs are fast dying out. Boys educated at a National School think it almost beneath their dignity to sing the ungrammatical, unrhythmical and unpoetical songs in which their fathers and forefathers delighted.' Frank Kidson, in Yorkshire, had the same fears: 'The old traditional songs are fast dying out, never to be recalled. They are now seldom or never sung, but rather *remembered*, by old people.' In 1905 Baring-Gould told Sharp that 'without a single exception, all his old singers have gone to their long rest,' and Sharp himself declared that 'the last generation of folk singers

22

must have been born not later than sixty or seventy years ago — say 1840.'

All this added to the excitement of the hunt, and probably no one who has discovered folksong for himself has been immune from this sense of mild panic in case it disappears. But while it was true that Baring-Gould, Sharp, Gardiner and the others often returned to check a song, only to find the singer dead, their desperation was misplaced; there are still songs to be collected today, and there will be some left tomorrow.

The rural areas in which the collectors predominantly worked were indeed in decline. Devon, in particular, was being depopulated at an alarming rate, whole villages becoming virtually deserted except for the old and the lame, as younger and fitter families moved away to the towns or to Canada or New Zealand. It was not surprising that there was an air of gloom and change for the worse among those that were left. But perhaps Sharp was relying too much on the old people's memories of the 'good old days', or perhaps he was just sentimentalising, when he wrote that 'old country people... all repeat the same tale. Everyone sang in their young days, they will tell you. They went to their work in the mornings singing; they sang in the fields, and they trudged home in the evenings to the accompaniment of song.' However, although agriculture in England was in a depressed state around 1900, it had scarcely been any better sixty or so years before.

If what most of the collectors seem to suggest — that their singers had to dredge in their memories of forty or more years before — is true, then some of them must have had remarkable recall. Sharp said that he had taken down as many as a hundred genuine folksongs from a single singer, and to note thirty or forty was commonplace. Henry Burstow, one of Lucy Broadwood's Sussex singers, claimed to know four hundred songs and had, he said, once sung them to a gentleman, taking a month to do it. But not all the singers were so forthcoming. George Gardiner, who had the idea of combing the workhouses for possible singers and visited seventeen in Wiltshire alone, told a story about an old woman at one workhouse who hid under the bedclothes, believing that he had come to kill her. He lured her out with peppermints, after which she sang three songs for him. (Sometimes he was given gifts in return. He came back from one collecting trip with a cucumber.) Baring-Gould, too, had his difficulties. Having contacted an old man in a cottage at Princetown on Dartmoor and taken down some songs, he returned next day for some more and was confronted by the man's wife. 'What do you mean by coming here and getting my 'usband to zing his drashy old songs,' she cried, 'when he ought to be preparing to meet his Saviour? No, you shan't see him. He's in bed and shall remain there. I've took his trousers and burnt 'em.' On another occasion, Baring-Gould lent another old man a book of broadsides. When he called again, the old man's wife and daughter threatened to burn the book unless he took it away; they had been kept awake all night by the old man's singing.

But the collectors of the pre-1914 era were wrong in thinking that they had heard folksong's dying gasps. About the time of the founding of the Folk Song Society, a young man called Harry Cox was growing up in Norfolk. 'I have been hungry, used to eat turnips sometimes,' he recalled later. 'I was about seventeen, got about 9s 6d (47½p), paid 7s (35p) for my board, done all farm-work.' By Sharp's definition of a true folksinger he was thirty-five years too young and, what is more, had been corrupted by the National School. But his was a singing family, and he claimed to be able to trace some of his songs two centuries back through his grandparents and their grandparents. He was 'discovered' as a folk singer in 1921, when he was thirty-six, by the Anglo-Irish collector and composer E. J. Moeran. He made the first of many recordings in the early 1930s, when two of his songs came out on a 78 rpm record, and he went on later, until his death in 1971, to make innumerable recordings both for the BBC archive and for commercial issue.

An even more striking example of the fact that folk singing remained a live art long after the early collectors were pronouncing doom is that of Fred Jordan. He was born in 1922, two years before Cecil Sharp's death and fifteen years after Sharp had urged fellow members of the Folk Song Society to hurry or they would be too late. Fred Jordan, who has spent his working life on the farm, was thirty years old when Peter Kennedy, touring Shropshire on a song-hunting expedition for the BBC archive, found him – a man still singing in the traditional style, evidently not having been tempted to adapt himself to a more contemporary idiom which would have earned him a readier reception from, say, pub audiences. Fred Jordan's songs were a mixture of traditional pieces such as *We're all jolly fellows that follow the plough* and *John Barleycorn*, which he had learned either from his parents or from gypsies visiting the area for seasonal work, and Victorian ballads and music-hall songs which he sang in the folk way. Yet he had not been born when Cecil Sharp was writing of the last link being forged in the chain of tradition!

Even today, an old man or woman could have picked up in childhood, from grandparents, songs that were current in the childhood of those grandparents – that is, not far removed from Sharp's dividing line of 1840. And it may be that Sharp and his fellow collectors misread the reluctance of the old men and women to come forward with their songs. It may not have been that singing was dead, but merely that it was thought not to be of interest to middle-class enquirers. The squire and parson Baring-

Gould, the prickly intellectual Sharp, the retired colonial civil servant Hammond and the classics scholar Gardiner must have had great difficulty in conveying to their contacts what they wanted. Sharp, at least, refers to this problem. In *English Folk Song: Some Conclusions* he remarks that most singers know a certain number of 'composed' songs and goes on: 'Indeed, it is these songs that they will offer first to the collector in the mistaken belief that, like all educated people, he will prefer them to the old fashioned songs'. And again: 'It is, as a rule, only waste of time to call upon singers under the age of sixty. Their songs are nearly all modern; if, by chance, they happen to sing an old one, it is so infected with the modern spirit that it is hardly worth the gathering.'

Harry Cox and Fred Jordan, who are only two of the dozens of genuine folk singers to have emerged since Sharp's time, prove him wrong. Anyone interested in collecting folksongs today should note that Cecil Sharp — like his colleagues — was far too pessimistic.

4. Collecting in the age of recording

Between the wars

It was unfortunate for folksong collectors and birdsong record-ists — though good luck for most other people — that the brief bat-tle between wax cylinders and disc recording, fought between rival companies in the years preceding the First World War, was won by disc recording. It was possible to take wax cylinder recording into the field, and, as we have seen, Percy Grainger among others did so. But disc recording was cumbersome and time-consuming, requiring a pantechnicon full of equipment, and so it could not be done by amateurs; while recording companies themselves were only rarely prepared to undertake it. For many years, they would not do so in an area of minority interest like folksong.

In Britain, only a handful of genuine folksongs were issued commercially on record up to the end of the Second World War, and these recordings were made in the studio. This tiny output is an accurate reflection of the amount of field recording that was being done. Meanwhile, the age of the parson collectors and of professional musical interest in folksong had passed; such interest as remained tended to be academic and to concentrate on the literary ballads.

If Sharp had lived into the 1930s he might well have thought that folksong's dark night, which he had prophesied, had come. Following the amalgamation of the Folk Song Society and the English Folk Dance Society in 1932, dance seemed to be in the ascendant, fitting in so well with the inter-war demand for healthy physical activity, with the social lives of rambling and hiking groups and with group camps and holiday camps. The lamentable vogue for 'community singing' encouraged by the Scout and other youth movements (and given public blessing by King George VI when he was Duke of York) did nothing to help the cause of folksong.

In the 1920s Frank Kidson, in collaboration with Alfred Mof-fatt, published three new collections of songs, but these were based on his pre-war work and suffered from heavy rewriting. About the only serious collector at work after the First World War was Alfred Williams, whose interest, in texts only, was fairly short-lived. Williams was a self-taught hammerman who spent twenty-five years at the Swindon railway works, learning languages and writing in his scant spare time — he worked an eleven-hour day, with in addition four-mile walks to and from work — before he left in 1914, broken by the job. He began collect-ing song texts in Wiltshire and Gloucestershire, publishing them in the local paper for a fee of 3d a song. Some of these were later published in book form as *Folk Songs of the Upper Thames*

(1923), but after this Williams seems to have had some argument with the Folk Song Society which disenchanted him with collecting. (A certain amount of tetchiness seems to go with folksong collecting; Cecil Sharp was certainly difficult, and so was Frank Kidson.) Williams collected in the Edwardian way, travelling by bicycle and taking down texts in longhand. He died in 1930, having transferred his interest to Sanskrit, but almost two hundred songs collected by him are held in the Swindon public library. He rediscovered much that Sharp and his colleagues had found a decade or more before, but he was not as selective as Sharp, and so his collection is interesting as a record of what country people actually *were* singing, including a number of derivatives of 'vulgar street songs', in the period 1914-21 rather than what someone – for example, Sharp – might think that they *should* be singing.

This effort of Williams's apart (and most of it was completed by 1920), the inter-war period was a dispiriting time for those interested in English folksong. In the United States, however, there were two developments which were later to be copied in Britain to good effect. As early as 1927, despite the physical difficulties of field recording described earlier, the RCA Victor company sent a mobile recording unit into the mountain communities of Kentucky, Tennessee and West Virginia, recording country singers and instrumentalists in miners' clubs and village halls. The fruits of this expedition confirmed what Cecil Sharp had found earlier on his American travels – that a good deal of folksong had been carried across the Atlantic by English migrants and had taken on a life of its own in the United States. It was possible to relate some of this material more closely to its ballad origins than the English versions which had been corrupted – as Sharp would have put it – by the intervention of broadside printers. The commercial results of the RCA Victor project included the 1930s craze for 'hillbilly' music, the vogue for singing cowboys, and eventually the development of popular country and western music. Radio was well established in the United States by this time, and it was a surprise to the recording companies that, despite the blandishments of city singers of *I love my wife, but oh you kid* or *Hello Central, give me heaven*, the mountain people seemed to prefer the old songs their mothers had taught them, for which no sheet music or records needed to be bought. (The record companies and radio networks soon changed that; within a couple of years the country and western industry had been born.) But the relevance of the RCA Victor experiment to folksong collecting in England – or, for that matter, anywhere else in the developed world – was that it demonstrated the richness of the material available to an organisation equipped to retrieve it. However, collecting on a professional basis for commercial use outside the United States had to await the invention of the tape recorder.

Meanwhile, in the 1930s the Library of Congress – perhaps in-spired by the RCA Victor project, and certainly covering much the same ground, though more carefully and with a more academic approach – began a programme of folksong recording in the field. This in turn stimulated interest in folksong among American universities, something which certainly did not exist in British universities at that time. But the Library of Congress pro-ject found a parallel in Britain when, during the Second World War, the BBC began, on a modest scale, to record country singers and musicians in the field. The project began in the West Country (perhaps following the lead of the early collectors), and the fact that Richard Dimbleby, then a BBC war correspondent, was responsible for some recordings suggests that these sessions pro-vided light relief for some of the Corporation's more battle-scarred staff. From this beginning, the BBC's folk music and dialect recording scheme of the early post-war years grew, record-ing both known and unknown singers. Some of the material and performers discovered were subsequently used in such pro-grammes as *Country Magazine*, and later in a long-running Sunday morning series *As I Roved Out*. Regrettably, the BBC tended to lose interest in folk music after about the mid 1950s, but the substantial archive it built up still exists and a few items have been issued commercially.

By now, tape recording was freely available, becoming pro-gressively easier to manage as machines became more portable, and this spurred a new wave of interest among both amateurs and, for example, the staff of the English Folk Dance and Song Society, who made field-recording forays. As the amount of col-lecting again increased, so did the general interest in folksong, and this in turn led to the revival.

The revival

Country singers tend to be old, forgetful and not always in good voice. If they forget the words or the tune, they are likely to make up something to fit. They make no distinction – as Sharp was irritated to find – between genuine folksong, half-remembered Victorian ballads of the *Don't go down the mine* sort, and popular songs of their childhood. Also, for many people interested in folksong, and certainly for those coming new to it, field recordings make difficult listening.

One of the problems of folksong collecting has always been how to make it accessible to a wider audience once it has been rediscovered. Taking the place of Cecil Sharp's school ar-rangements and Vaughan Williams's hymn books, the guitar has today become the standard 'carrier'. If folksong is to flourish within the body of music as a whole, it must observe current musical conventions, hence 'the revival' – the transcription of songs in terms that listeners without a musical education can accept and enjoy.

By the end of the 1950s revival singers were to be heard in folk clubs, usually held in the upstairs rooms of pubs, up and down Britain, and the growth of university education in the 1960s also strengthened this side of the movement. People brought into contact with folk sound by listening to protest singers such as Bob Dylan and Joan Baez stayed on to appreciate genuine folksong. The audience had now grown sufficiently to support a number of commercial record companies, while other companies issued occasional folk music recordings. The peak of all this activity was in the early 1970s, since when it has declined to some extent, but — those few years apart — it has never been easier to listen to folk singers in person, buy their records or follow up folksong in print.

We have learned that Sharp was being pessimistic when he wrote in 1907 that it was 'of the highest importance that not only the songs, but that all things that relate to the art of folksinging, should be accurately recorded while there is yet time and opportunity'. But it has to be admitted that it is less easy than it was in his time (and it was not especially easy then) to find the singers. Television and the price of beer keep them at home in the evening, and many of the pubs where they used to be found have either closed or been smartened up for more affluent trade. The typical singer's pub will probably look rather run down outside, with basic furniture and interior decor and almost certainly rather warm beer.

A hunting ground for collectors which has not been explored as thoroughly as it might be is the factory sports and social club, especially in the older established industries. Company clubs often run special pensioners' afternoons and evenings, and in this informal atmosphere it is possible to stir memories and pick up a song or two.

5. A folksong alphabet

As I walked out one midsummer's morning is a first line that countless folksongs have in common. Nearly all songs starting this way go on to tell a tale of seduction or attempted seduction, often of the wicked squire and the milkmaid sort, though sometimes with the roles reversed.

One huge family of *As I walked out* songs is descended from a long ballad of 1609 called *The baffled knight, or lady's policy*, which was one of those collected by Samuel Pepys. This begins with a drunken knight meeting a fine lady on his morning ride. By verse two, he is suggesting that they should lie down on the grass. In the original ballad, which runs to one hundred and eighty verses, she engages in a series of tricks to preserve her honour, ending by inviting the knight into her castle by way of a plank that she had laid across the moat. The plank, previously almost sawn through, snaps and the knight gets a ducking.

After 1609, the ballad seems to have led two different lives. In one, it went on being sung in its original form – though much shortened – until it emerged from the notebooks of Cecil Sharp and the Hammond brothers as *Blow away the morning dew*. Most versions had lost the knight drunk with wine, however, and substituted a 'brisk young farmer' and had attracted an 'As I walked out' opening. The common link, though, is the theme of woman's guile.

Blacksmiths were popular folksong heroes. Perhaps because of their characteristic physique, or because of the usefulness of the hammer and anvil as sexual symbols, they had a reputation for ardour and staying power which earned them a place in many a song. The best known blacksmith song is *Twankydillo*, though readers who know only the school version will be surprised to read the words originally collected by Baring-Gould and others, though Hammond, collecting at Mosterton in Dorset, found the final verse 'too indecent to write down'. A gentler blacksmith is portrayed in *A blacksmith courted me*, though he lets his girl down by joining the army. One version of this song was collected in Herefordshire by Vaughan Williams, who later used the tune as the basis of *Monksgate*, the familiar setting of Bunyan's hymn 'To be a pilgrim'.

The cruel mother (sometimes listed as *Down by the greenwood side*, *The lady from Lee*, *There was a lady lived in York*, among other titles) is straight from the folk-tale world of wicked stepmothers, hauntings and curses. As usual in folksong, details vary between different versions, but the basic story is the same. The cruel mother stabs her two illegitimate children at birth. Later, when she has married and is living in some state, they haunt her. She describes the life they would lead if they were hers again: fine silks, white bread and wine. They remind her of how she treated them when they were born and sentence her to hell.

The origin of this song seems to have been a broadside printed in 1690, and a very popular one it must have been. Versions have been found all over England and Scotland, and on Cecil Sharp's collecting tours of North America he discovered an almost unaltered version in the Kentucky Mountains. But perhaps the most remarkable tribute to the durability of the song – or, at least, its story – is that it has survived, without any help from the folksong revival, as a children's skipping rhyme (*There was an old woman and she lived in a wood*) which is still sung in streets and playgrounds.

Dives and Lazarus is one of the oldest folksong tunes, and its life has certainly been varied as well as long. Many readers will know it as *The star of the County Down*, though this was a composed song written in the 1920s for the Irish tenor John McCormack. Earlier, it had been used as the setting for a much loved nineteenth-century carol, *Come all you worthy Christian men*, which included a retelling of the story of the beggar Lazarus from Luke 16. So the tune got its usual name, though it is clearly much older. It is the tune of *John Barleycorn*, a song of great antiquity.

Writing in 1859, the collector and publisher William Chappell described *Dives and Lazarus* as the tune 'most frequently heard in the streets of London'. Among the verses sung to it were the stories of Maria Marten, murdered in the Red Barn, and of the great prizefight in 1824 between the Irish American Paddy Heenan and the English champion Tom Sayers.

The elfin knight is the name given to another of the great families of folksongs. The theme is of a girl setting her man a series of riddles, with herself as the prize. Almost everyone has heard at least one version, *I gave my love a cherry without a stone*, and another, *Are you going to Scarborough Fair?*, is nearly as well known. The original ballad – at the least, from the seventeenth century, and probably earlier – is about a series of riddles posed by 'the laird of Rosslyn's daughter' to 'Captain Wedderburn, a soldier of the king'. The cherry without a stone appears in this version, together with other riddles which survived the song's many transformations. Having solved all the riddles, the Captain gets his girl.

Floating verses, in folksong, are verses that occur in a number of songs without any apparent connection with the story. Old-time audiences tended to like a song with plenty of verses, partly because it gave them a better opportunity to learn the tune, and floating verses were a useful way of 'padding'. Two typical floating verses are:

31

Love is teasing and love is pleasing,
And love is charming when it's new;
But love grows colder as it grows older
And fades away like the morning dew.

I wish, I wish but 'tis all in vain,
I wish I was a maid again.
But a maid again I'll never be
Till apples grow on an orange tree.

Gallows songs, printed for sale at public executions, were a popular form of broadside until public hanging was abolished in the mid nineteenth century. These events attracted great crowds — there were said to be seven thousand people at the hanging of William Corder, the murderer of Maria Marten — and provided an eager market for broadside sellers. The trade was flourishing by the middle of the seventeenth century, when one best seller told the tale of George Barnwell, who was set up to rob and murder his girlfriend's uncle.

There must have been hundreds, perhaps thousands, of gallows songs telling the stories of murderers, pirates, traitors and other felons. They fulfilled a similar role to that of today's more sensational Sunday newspapers, and when more popular newspapers came on the market from the mid nineteenth century, gallows songs faded away, though many went on being sung in oral tradition. Some were noted by the early collectors, who tended to reject them as 'vulgar'.

The handsome cabin boy is a widely collected song written round the popular idea of a girl who stows away to sea to be near her sailor lover. There are similar army versions. The song is unusual in that although it was collected by Sharp, Baring-Gould and others in various parts of the West Country, words and tune were almost identical. This may be a tribute to the popularity of the story line. There were several well known examples of women who did go to sea dressed as men, but the girl in the song is always anonymous.

Innkeepers figure prominently in folksong, usually as unsympathetic characters with time only for a man with money in his pocket. In the sailors' song *Homeward bound*, a vivid profile of dockland life in mid Victorian times, the innkeeper is called 'Grouser', with a smile of welcome for sailors coming ashore and a frown when their money has gone. In *The wild rover* an innkeeper is brutally short with the roving man who asks for credit: 'Such a custom as yours I could have every day,' she says. In the recruiting song *The rout of the Blues*, the innkeeper stands hopefully by with a bottle of gin as the recruiting sergeant hands out the King's Shilling.

Joan's ale (sometimes *Jones's ale*), however, presents landladies (or perhaps brewers) in a better light. This is a rather hearty number much sung in folk clubs when the audience is invited to join in, and at first sight seems to belong with the 'real ale' revival. But it first appeared (as *Jones's ale*) on a broadside of 1579 and seems to have been in circulation ever since. Probably its attraction is its amenability to having extra verses added on. 'The first to come in was a soldier/With a flintlock on his shoulder.' one Cecil Sharp version began, and it went on through a mason, a tailor, a dyer, a hatter, a tinker and a ragman; and so the song could go on through all trades and occupations until the singer's stamina or rhyming ability failed.

The keys of heaven has a stranger history. It is related to *O no John*, to which Sharp did some disservice by providing a sugary piano accompaniment and a vapid, romantic text. (As noted down, he said, the song was 'coarse and needed considerable revision'. It is as well that he did not survive to hear the version commonly sung in rugby clubs.) In *O no John* the man has the major singing part, the women contributing only the last line of each verse. In *The keys of heaven* (also known as *The keys of the kingdom* or *The keys of Canterbury*) the man and woman have alternate verses to themselves. The man offers various gifts – a pair of gloves, a new silk gown, boots of cork, and so on – and the woman rejects them until he offers her 'the key of my heart', when she accepts him. (In some more cynical versions, she accepts only when she is offered 'a purse of gold', and is then properly rejected by her suitor.)

This song has been collected so frequently in so many different versions that one would have thought it must have a traceable origin; but collectors have so far been unable to find it. One writer, James Reeves, suggests that it began as a singing game. However that may be, it passed easily across the Atlantic with the English settlers and was collected widely in the United States, with many of the gifts the same as in the English version. However, at some time before the First World War the theme was used for a sickly parlour ballad (*Madam, will you walk?*), and this version, too, has its descendants in oral song. Evidently, the theme was a popular one.

Lovely Joan was a girl of the same way of thinking, evidently, as the heroine of *Blow away the morning dew*. (Indeed, the song may be yet another descendant of the same original ballad.) Meeting a 'fine young man' one day, she accepted a ring as payment, in advance, for lying in the hay with him. As he dismounted from his horse, she climbed on it and rode away with the ring to 'her true love's gate'. Vaughan Williams was among the collectors who noted this song – at Acle in Norfolk – and he used the tune as the second theme in his well known *Greensleeves* arrangement.

Maria Marten's murder in 1827 by William Corder, her seducer, caught the public imagination in an astonishing way, considering that it happened before the days of popular newspapers. It was not until the following year that Corder was arrested, after Maria's mother had had three dreams in which she saw Corder shooting her daughter and burying her body in the Red Barn. When Corder was hanged at Bury St Edmunds, over seven thousand people went to watch and later to file past his body. A broadside — only one of many — about the murder and trial is said to have sold well over a million copies, and so it is not surprising that versions of Maria Marten songs have been discovered in the repertoire of country singers. The best known of these, *Maria and William*, collected by the Hammonds in 1905, romanticises the story considerably. Maria becomes 'a girl of high degree' (in fact, she had had two illegitimate children before meeting Corder), the motive becomes jealousy and the murder weapon poison.

The Norfolk gent was the original title of a ballad first printed about 1600 with a story known better as the pantomime *The Babes in the Wood*. The villain is the uncle of two orphaned children, and he murders them for the sake of their inheritance. The original ballad is twenty verses long and ends with the wicked uncle ruined by 'the heavy wrath of God'.

In the middle of the eighteenth century, *The Spectator* described *The Norfolk gent* as 'one of the darling songs of the common people'. A much shorter version, by then called *The babes in the wood*, was collected in Sussex in the early years of the twentieth century. Both this version and the original include the incident familiar from the pantomime, in which robins cover the bodies of the children with leaves. There is an interesting confirmation of the historical basis of the story. Griston Hall, near Watton in Norfolk, is said to have been the home of the wicked uncle, and nearby Wayland Wood is reputed to be haunted by the ghosts of the two children as they wander about crying and looking for a way out.

The outlandish knight is another of the great ballad songs, and not only in England; according to the folklorist A. L. Lloyd, versions of the story exist all over Europe as well as in French Canada. This is another story of a cheated seducer. The outlandish knight (outlandish because he comes from another part of the country, not because he looks extraordinary, as in the modern sense of the word) promises to marry the girl if she will go away with him, bringing her parents' gold and jewels. They ride away on her father's two best horses. When they reach the sea, the knight tells the girl that he is going to kill her for her money, just as he has killed six others. (Some scholars have noted a Bluebeard parallel here.) He tells her to take off her dress so that he can sell it, but she orders him to look away while she undresses. Attacking him from behind, she throws him into the sea, and, leading the knight's horse, rides home. Although the song has been so widely collected, its English versions are remarkably consistent and seem to come from a broadside published about 1800.

Poaching in eighteenth- and nineteenth-century England was, for many rural families, the only means of survival, and no one except the squires and their gamekeepers believed it to be a crime. There were many tales of how poachers outwitted or outran the keepers, and some of these found their way into folksong. The best known, ruined by too much use in schools, is *The Lincolnshire Poacher*. Unfortunately, many poaching songs must have disappeared without trace, because broadside printers, on the whole, tended to be on the side of law and order.

Quête songs are begging songs, of which the best known survivor is *We wish you a merry Christmas*. They were often sung at the end of a play like *St George and the Dragon*, before the collection was taken. Included in this group are wassail songs, sung from house to house at midwinter, and it was natural enough that when this custom became Christianised as carol singing, many of the old tunes became used for Christian carols. Examples are *God rest ye merry, gentlemen* and the Cornish setting of *While shepherds watched*.

Royalty rarely features in folksong. Songs of the 'Here's a health unto His Majesty' type were almost always composed by court hacks, and ignored by most people. However, one royal death, that of Jane Seymour, evidently caught the imagination of the public, for *The death of Queen Jane* survived long enough to be collected by Hammond in 1907, and by others. Popular memory preferred a romantic deathbed scene to the historical truth, and the song has Jane pleading for her right side to be opened so that the baby, at least, will live. A reluctant Henry VIII finally agrees, and Jane dies. In truth, the birth of the future Edward VI was normal, and his mother died about a fortnight later.

Sea-songs make up a huge category of folksongs, and there are many sea-songs which are not folk at all, though often described as such. *Rule Britannia!*, *Hearts of oak* and similar songs were composed, some of them by a song writer employed by the Admiralty for some years to compose recruiting songs. True sea-songs dating from the age of sail are divided into two groups: shanties (for example, *Blow the man down*), which were sung as an accompaniment to work and to help it along, and forebitters, which were songs for entertainment, sung in the forecastle when the men were off watch. Shanties were led by a shantyman, who would start with a basic song and make up his own words as he went along, so it follows that there are scores of different sets of words for any given shanty tune. Forebitters were often about adventures at sea, though some were based on broadsides or country songs. One favourite was *Homeward bound*, which contrasts the welcome given by dockyard girls and landlords to sailors coming ashore with their pay, and their attitude when the money has gone.

The trees they grow so high (sometimes called *Young but growing* or *Still growing*) has been described by A. L. Lloyd in the *Penguin Book of English Folk Songs* as 'one of the most curious, most beautiful and most widespread of British ballads'. It is the story of a girl (her age is variously given as anywhere between twelve and fifteen) whose father arranges a marriage with a younger boy. The boy is sent away to school, but he dies, leaving the girl to lie alone and mourn. The theme of child marriage (and a verse about the couple going into a hayfield, after which 'she never more complained of his growing') made this a sensitive song for early collectors, as a result of which it escaped piano arrangement and survives intact today. Sharp, Baring-Gould and others found innumerable versions, all very similar, and it seems likely that all came from one widely distributed broadside.

The unquiet grave is another of the treasures of English folksong and could almost be a sequel to *The trees they grow so high*. Twelve months after the death of her lover, a girl is mourning by his graveside. His ghost protests: she must stop mourning so that he can rest. This is another song which was widely collected during the 1890s and 1900s, though with a variety of tunes and many different versions of the text. All have in common, however, the distinctive first verse:

> Cold blows the wind tonight, my love,
> > Cold are the drops of rain.
> The very first love that ever I had
> > In the cold grave he is lain.

Van Dieman's Land (Tasmania) was first colonised by the British in 1803. In 1807 the first convicts, transported from Britain, arrived, and thousands more were to follow — fifteen thousand in four years alone — until 1853, when the transportation system was abolished. Many of the prisoners were from the English shires, convicted of such rural offences as poaching and sheep stealing, and the effect on them of being dumped on an island where the aborigines were hostile and the planters treated their workers like cattle can be imagined. A bitter folksong, *Van Dieman's Land*, is based on a broadside published in London about 1830 and lived on in country districts until the twentieth century.

The song **Waly waly** shows how mysterious the ways of folksong can be, and how much detective work is needed to sort them out. The story begins in Scotland in 1681, when Lord James

36

Douglas disowned his wife Barbara, whom he had married eleven years earlier, on information from his chamberlain that she had committed adultery. A ballad in which Lady Barbara laments her lost love appeared not very long after, and a long central section consisted of a series of verses such as:

> I put my hand into the bush
> Thinking the sweetest flower to find,
> I pricked my finger to the bone
> And left the sweetest flower alone.

Some of these central verses, however, seem to have strayed from an earlier ballad published over a century before the break-up of the marriage, and again, as the song has passed from singer to singer, other floating verses have been added. At the same time, the Scottish context of the original has been lost (perhaps as the song moved south) and in England *Waly waly* is usually a generalised young girl's lament for her lost lover. The 1765 collection of Thomas Percy includes a version from which all the Scottishness has been removed; Percy's note says, 'This is a very ancient song, but we could only give it from a modern copy.' The result is that there are *two* songs known as *Waly waly*, one giving the Lord James Douglas and Lady Barbara story and the other, more common in England at least, containing only the laments. Cecil Sharp collected four versions of the latter in the West Country. But, to make matters more confusing, there is another song, usually called *Love is pleasing*, also collected in the West of England and well known in Scotland, which has some verses in common with *Waly waly*. It is possible that all these variants spring from one original ballad which has not been identified.

X was always a problem for compilers of alphabets, and so it was with those who made up 'alphabet songs'. These seem to have originated with a forebitter, *The sailor's alphabet*, which often included scurrilous couplets about the captain and the shipowners. Other trades and occupations took them over, suitably altering the words, and there was a vogue in Victorian times for political alphabets such as *The people's comic alphabet* and *The alphabet of old England*. The sailor's alphabet got round the *X* problem like this:

> W's the Wheel, at which we serve time,
> And the other three letters, they won't come in rhyme.

Another let-out was to make use of the formula 'if you want any more you can sing it yourself'.

The young man cut down in his prime (or young sailor, young soldier, young trooper, young maid, and so on) is a member of a huge family of folksongs whose theme, surprisingly, is venereal disease. The singer laments his fate and pleads for a ceremonial funeral, usually ending by urging others to take warning by his example. The origins are obscure, but it appeared (as *The unfortunate lad*) on a mid Victorian broadside which was the source of many of the versions collected some fifty years later. The song crossed the Atlantic and became *The cowboy's lament*, *The streets of Laredo* and *St James's Infirmary*.

Zoology features quite strongly in folksong, especially in songs about miraculous animals with remarkable powers. Perhaps the best known of these is *The Derby ram* ('The wool that grew on its back, sir/It covered five acres of ground') and its close relation *The Yorkshire tup*. Sailors have *The wonderful crocodile*, probably best known in England from one of its scabrous rugby versions. One reason for the strong survival of these nonsense songs is probably that they gave scope to inventive singers to add new verses of their own.

6. Finding out more

English Folk Dance and Song Society, 2 Regents Park Road, London NW1 7AY (telephone 01-485 2206).

Membership of the society is essential for anyone interested in English folksong whether as a student, collector or listener. The annual subscription is modest, and there are reduced rates for students, married couples, families and pensioners.

The society publishes an annual *Journal* (free to members), the annual *Folk Directory* (half-price to members) and, three times a year, the magazine *English Dance and Song*. The Vaughan Williams Memorial Library at the London headquarters houses nine thousand books on aspects of folk dance and song, together with magazines, manuscripts and other material. Members may borrow books. The Sound Library contains over 3,500 discs and tapes, mainly of British field recordings.

There are four regional offices (in Newmarket, Kettering, Leeds and Exeter) and county activities are organised on a voluntary basis. Records, books and instruments can be bought at the Folk Shop run by the society, through regional offices and sales representatives, and through Folk Mail, the Folk Shop's mail order service.

Folk clubs

There are several hundred folk clubs in England, usually meeting weekly (though not necessarily in summer) and often held in pubs or community halls. Like most organisations depending on the enthusiasm of a few people, folk clubs tend to wax and wane, and it is not practical to provide a list here since it would rapidly be out of date. However, *Folk Directory* includes an up-to-date annual list of clubs with details of their meetings. Some universities, polytechnics and other further education establishments have folk clubs which admit members of the general public. Details can be obtained from Students' Union offices.

Pubs

County secretaries of the EFDSS (listed in *Folk Directory*) should know of pubs in their areas which have folksong nights.

Folk holidays

The Western Region of the EFDSS organises folk holidays and weekends at its residential folk centre at Halsway Manor in the Quantock Hills.

Folk Camps Society Ltd, a subsidiary of the EFDSS, organises camps throughout the summer in a number of locations in the

United Kingdom and western Europe. Details from: 10 Richmond Road, Exeter, Devon, EX4 4JF (send a stamped addressed envelope).

Festivals

Folk festivals offer the opportunity to hear a wide range of folk music. Some festivals, like the clubs, come and go, but among the more enduring ones are:

May: Eastbourne, Holmfirth, Felixstowe, Chester, Cleethorpes, Lacock and Chippenham, Barnstaple.
June: Christchurch, South Petherton, Lichfield, Crawley, Reading.
July: Southend-on-Sea, Gloucester, Potterne, Loughborough, Redcar, Northumberland, Taunton, Sidmouth.
August: Durham, Broadstairs, Whitby, Kendal, Kettering.
September: Fleetwood, Waterlooville, Whitchurch (Hampshire).
October: West Yorkshire.

Further details appear in *Folk Directory* and *English Dance and Song*. The EFDSS's own annual Folk Festival — an afternoon or evening performance — is held in February at the Royal Albert Hall, London, and there are concessionary prices for members.

Magazines

Apart from the EFDSS's own publications, mentioned above, *Folk Review* (monthly; 19 Clark Road, Wolverhampton, WV3 9NP) is the only folk periodical of national standing in England.

Melody Maker (weekly; widely available from newsagents) gives good coverage of the current folk scene.

Books

It would be possible to fill a whole library with books on folksong (and the EFDSS has done it) but the following selection gives a good representative coverage of the field, starting with the essential book for anyone interested in the subject.

Folk Song in England, A. L. Lloyd (Lawrence and Wishart, hardback, 1967, Panther paperback 1969, Paladin paperback 1975). The standard work by Britain's leading expert on folk music, it ranges over the whole field, from balladry to industrial songs, quoting hundreds of musical and textual examples.
English Folk Song: *Some Conclusions*, Cecil Sharp (Mercury, 1965). As indicated earlier, this has its weaknesses but it is an illuminating account of the work of Sharp, sounder on tunes than words.
The Idiom of the People, James Reeves (Heinemann, 1958). A

40

detailed study (texts only) of the songs collected by Sharp,
quoting his original notebooks.

The Everlasting Circle, James Reeves (Heinemann, 1960). A
similar study of Baring-Gould, Hammond and Gardiner.

Folk Songs of the Upper Thames, Alfred Williams (EP reprint,
1970). Texts only, with some censorship by Williams.

Reliques of Ancient English Poetry, Thomas Percy (Dover, 1966).
A three-volume facsimile for the academically inclined, but
Percy, too, edited his material quite heavily.

English and Scottish Popular Ballads, Francis J. Child (Dover,
1966). In five volumes, this scholarly work traces the variants
and descent of the great ballads, though with few tunes.

Song books

Song books of interest to the reader contain words and tunes,
preferably as collected and certainly *without* piano arrangement,
though some indicate guitar chords. From a vast range, the
following are recommended:

The Seeds of Love (edited by Stephen Sedley). EFDSS/Essex
Music, 1967.

The Constant Lovers (edited by Frank Purslow). EFDSS, 1972.

The Foggy Dew (edited by Frank Purslow). EFDSS, 1974.

Marrow Bones (edited by Frank Purslow). EFDSS, 1965.

The Wanton Seed (edited by Frank Purslow). EFDSS, 1969.

The Penguin Book of English Folk Songs (edited by R. Vaughan
Williams and A. L. Lloyd). Penguin, 1959 and later editions.

Records

A large number of companies and individuals issue folksong
records, but many of these are transitory or limit themselves to
one artist or group, or distribute only through folk clubs.

The EFDSS issues a select list of records, some for members
only but others available to the general public. Details from the
Folk Shop, 2 Regents Park Road, London NW1 7AY.

Among the commercial companies, the leading folk music label
is Topic Records (50 Stroud Green Road, London N4 3EF),
whose catalogue is in itself an invaluable guide to the breadth of
material available on record. Topic's output includes both traditional and revival recordings, together with some series drawn
from the BBC archives.

Other companies with substantial folk output are Argo (Decca,
1 Rockley Road, London W14 ODE) and Transatlantic (Transatlantic, Logo, Xtra, 119 Wardour Street, London W1V 3TD).

Leader Sound (Leader, Trailer, 209 Rochdale Road, Greetland,
Halifax, West Yorkshire, HX4 8JE) has an important catalogue
of traditional and revival singers.

In London, the Folk Shop (2 Regents Park Road, NW1 7AY), Chappell's (50 New Bond Street, WC1), Collet's (186 Shaftesbury Avenue, WC2) and Dobell's (77 Charing Cross Road, WC2) are recommended browsing places for folk records. It is less easy in the provinces, but small specialist shops do exist, and the EFDSS's Folk Mail should not be forgotten. It is well worth looking at market stalls, cut-price record shops and larger branches of Boots and W. H. Smith for records which may be on sale for a relatively short period and may not appear in catalogues at all.

Some public libraries with record loan schemes include folk music in their collections.

Radio and television

On television, neither the BBC nor ITV show any sustained interest in folk music, though occasionally folk (or, more often, 'folksy') groups may be featured.

In radio, the BBC's poor performance in recent years is the more regrettable in view of the sterling work it did during the 1940s and early 1950s, described earlier. The vast archive accumulated during those years is still virtually unexploited. Meanwhile, the BBC broadcasts *Folk on 2* and, very occasionally, more serious folk music programmes on Radio 3; but, again, there is no continuing commitment.

Both BBC and independent local radio stations broadcast folk music programmes in some areas, but the budgets for these are often inadequate.

Archive material

Some readers may wish to delve into the printed sources of folksong. One of the most active collectors in this field in recent years has been Roy Palmer, who has unearthed much fascinating material on the social history of song by going through the envelopes and box-files in local libraries and museums. (His books resulting from this work include *A Touch on the Times*, Penguin 1974, *The Rambling Soldier*, Kestrel/Peacock 1977, and a series of books initially intended for school use and published by Cambridge University Press under the general title *Resources of Music*.)

Almost all local history libraries have some kind of collection of broadsides, though in some cases these may amount only to a few items. Local history librarians should, however, know of other collections in the area. The following public libraries are known to have substantial collections: Birmingham, Derby, Plymouth, Oldham, Manchester, Newcastle upon Tyne, Sheffield, and Worcester. In some areas, county (or borough) record offices may house broadside collections and enquiries should be made to county (or borough) archivists. Unfortunately, since local government reorganisation much of this material remains unredistributed; it is worth enquiring at the old county, county borough, borough, urban or rural district council offices, not only from personal interest but also because such enquiries may prevent the material from disappearing altogether.

Some local museums also have collections.

Bibliography and discography

In the listing that follows, a printed and recorded reference is given for almost all the songs referred to in earlier chapters. The two are not necessarily compatible as few songs have a text that can be described as definitive. Wherever possible, printed sources giving tunes as well as words have been chosen.

The first title given is a printed source, and the letters after it indicate whether words (W) or tune (T) or both are given. The second source is a disc. Some discs may have been deleted from manufacturers' catalogues but may still be available second-hand, through specialist shops or from public libraries on loan. Discs known to be still listed at the time of publication are indicated with an asterisk*.

The following abbreviations are used for printed sources:

FSE: Lloyd, A. L. *Folk Song in England*. Lawrence and Wishart, 1967/Panther, 1969/Paladin, 1975.
IP: Reeves, James. *The Idiom of the People*. Heinemann, 1958.
PBEFS: Vaughan Williams, R. and Lloyd, A. L. (editors). *The Penguin Book of English Folk Songs*. Penguin, 1959.
SL: Sedley, Stephen (editor). *The Seeds of Love*. Essex Music/EFDSS, 1967.

Most of the songs mentioned have been printed or recorded widely, but only one printed and one recorded reference has been given. As far as possible these have been chosen from a limited number of sources.

Admiral Benbow. *FSE* (W). *A Cut Above*; June Tabor; Topic 12TS410.
Are you going to Scarborough fair? See *Scarborough fair*.
Babes in the wood. Copper, Bob; *A Song for Every Season*; Heinemann, 1971/Paladin, 1975 (WT). *The Sweet Primeroses*; Shirley Collins; Topic 12TS170.
Banks of green willow, The. *PBEFS* (WT). (As *The watery grave*) *Songs of a Shropshire Farm Worker*; Fred Jordan; Topic 12T150.

Blacksmith courted me, A. *PBEFS* (WT). *Heroes in Love*; Shirley Collins; Topic TOP95.

Blow away the morning dew. *SL* (WT). (As *The baffled knight*) **Folk Songs of Britain Volume 5*; Topic 12T161.

Blow the man down. Hugill, Stan; *Shanties and Sailors' Songs*; Herbert Jenkins, 1969 (WT). **Sea Songs and Shanties*; Topic TPS205.

Brigg Fair. O'Shaughnessy, Patrick; *Twenty-one Lincolnshire Folk Songs*; Novello, 1968 (WT). **The Sweet Primeroses*; Shirley Collins; Topic 12TS170.

Broken token, The. See *Claudy Banks*, *Dark-eyed sailor*, *Fair maid walking in her garden*.

Bushes and briars. *SL* (WT). (As *The bramble brier*) *Ballads and Broadsides*; Louis Killen; Topic 12T126.

Claudy Banks. Copper, Bob; *A Song for Every Season*; Heinemann, 1971/Paladin, 1975 (WT). **When the Frost is on the Pumpkin*; Fred Jordan; Topic 12TS233.

Come all you worthy Christian men. Sharp, Cecil J.; *English Folk Carols*; Novello, 1911 (WT). **All Bells in Paradise*; The Valley Folk; Topic 12T192.

Cruel mother, The. *PBEFS* (WT). **The Sweet Primeroses*; Shirley Collins; Topic 12TS170.

Dark-eyed sailor, The. Pollard, Michael (editor); *Ballads and Broadsides*; Pergamon, 1969 (W). Discs listed under *Claudy Banks* and *Fair maid walking in her garden*.

Death of Queen Jane, The. *PBEFS* (WT). *The Lark in the Morning*; Dave and Toni Arthur; Topic 12T190.

Derby ram, The. *IP* (W). **Adieu to Old England*; Shirley Collins; Topic 12TS238.

Dives and Lazarus. *FSE* (T). *Folk Songs of Britain Volume 9*; Topic 12T197.

Down by the greenwood side. See *Cruel mother*.

Elfin knight, The. (As *Captain Wedderburn's courtship*) *SL* (WT). **Folk Songs of Britain Volume 4*; Topic 12T160.

Faithful sailor, The. See *Claudy Banks*, *Dark-eyed sailor*, *Fair maid walking in her garden*.

Fair maid walking in her garden, A. (As *The young and single sailor*) *PBEFS* (WT). *The Rout of the Blues*; Robin and Barry Dransfield; Trailer LER 2011.

Fine old English gentleman, A. Chilton, Charles; *Victorian Folk Songs*; Essex Music, 1965 (WT). **Oldham's Burning Sands*; The Oldham Tinkers; Topic 12TS206.

Handsome cabin boy, The. *SL* (WT). (As *The female cabin boy*) **Songs from Suffolk*; Bob Hart; Topic 12TS225.

Hard times of old England, The. Copper, Bob; *A Song for Every Season*; Heinemann, 1971/Paladin, 1975 (WT). **Bob and Ron Copper*; EFDSS, LP 1002.

Homeward bound. (As *Outward bound*) Leaflet enclosed with
record (W). *Sweet Thames Flow Softly*; The Critics Group;
Argo ZDA 47.
I gave my love a cherry without a stone. See *Elfin knight*.
Jim the carter lad. Pollard, Michael (editor); *Ballads and Broad-
sides*; Pergamon, 1969 (W). No disc.
Joan's ale. (As *When Jones's ale was new*) Copper, Bob; *A Song
for Every Season*; Heinemann, 1971/Paladin, 1975 (WT).
When the Frost is on the Pumpkin; Fred Jordan; Topic
12TS233.
John Barleycorn. *PBEFS* (WT). *Frost and Fire*; The Watersons;
Topic 12T136.
Jones's ale. See *Joan's ale*.
Keep your feet still, Geordie hinny. Wilson, Joe; *Tyneside Songs
and Drolleries*; EP Publishing, reprint 1970 (WT). *Along
the Coaly Tyne*; Louis Killen and Johnny Handle; Topic
12T189.
Keys of heaven, The. *IP* (W). No disc.
Lady from Lee. See *Cruel mother*.
London mourning in ashes. Pollard, Michael (editor); *Ballads
and Broadsides*; Pergamon, 1969 (W). *A Merry Progress to
London*; The Critics Group; Argo ZDA 46.
Love is pleasing. *SL* (WT). *The Dubliners*; Transatlantic TRA
116.
Lovely Joan. *PBEFS* (WT). *The Power of the True Love Knot*;
Shirley Collins; Polydor 583 025.
Maria and William. *IP* (W). (As *Maria Marten*) *When Sheep-
shearing's Done*; Topic 12T254.
O no John. *SL* (WT). *Folk Songs of Britain Volume 1*; Topic
12T157.
Outlandish knight, The. *PBEFS* (WT). *The Moon Shone Bright*;
The Broadside; Topic 12TS228.
People's comic alphabet. Palmer, Roy; *A Touch on the Times*;
Penguin, 1974 (WT). No disc.
Poverty knock. *FSE* (WT). *The Bitter and the Sweet*; Roy Harris;
Topic 12TS217.
Roast beef of old England. See *Hard times of old England*.
Rout of the Blues, The. *IP* (W). *The Rout of the Blues*; Robin
and Barry Dransfield; Trailer LER 2011.
Sailor's alphabet, The. (As *The bosun's alphabet*) Hugill, Stan;
Shanties and Sailors' Songs; Herbert Jenkins, 1969 (WT). *A
Sailor's Garland*; Ewan MacColl and A. L. Lloyd; Transatlan-
tic XTRA 5013.
Scarborough fair. Leaflet enclosed with record (W). *The Long
Harvest*; Ewan MacColl and Peggy Seeger; Argo ZDA 67.
Seeds of love, The. *SL* (WT). *When the Frost is on the Pump-
kin*; Fred Jordan; Topic 12TS233.

Still growing. See *Trees they grow so high*.

Strawberry fair. Reeves, James; *The Everlasting Circle*; Heinemann, 1960 (W). No disc.

There was a lady lived in York. See *Cruel mother*.

Trees they grow so high, The. (As *Still growing*) *SL* (WT). *The Rout of the Blues*; Robin and Barry Dransfield; Trailer LER 2011.

Twankydillo. Copper, Bob; *A Song for Every Season*; Heinemann, 1971/Paladin, 1975 (WT). *The Watersons; Topic 12T142.

Unfortunate lad, The. See *Young man cut down in his prime*.

Unquiet grave, The. *SL* (WT). *The Power of the True Love Knot*; Shirley Collins; Polydor 583 205.

Van Dieman's Land. Palmer, Roy (editor); *The Painful Plough*; Cambridge University Press, 1973 (WT). *Folk Songs of Britain Volume 7*; Topic 12T195.

Villikins and Dinah. Chilton, Charles; *Victorian Folk Songs*; Essex Music, 1965 (WT). (Tune only, as *We're all jolly fellows that follow the plough*) *Folksound of Britain*; EMI/HMV CLP 1910.

Waly waly. *SL* (WT). *Airs and Graces; June Tabor; Topic 12TS298.

Wonderful crocodile, The. Palmer, Roy (editor); *Room for Company*; Cambridge University Press, 1972 (WT). *Room for Company*; Topic IMP-S-104.

Yorkshire tup, The. No printed source. **A Yorkshire Garland*; The Watersons; Topic 12T167.

Young but growing. See *Trees they grow so high*.

Young man cut down in his prime, The. (As *The young sailor cut down in his prime*) Purslow, Frank (editor); *Marrow Bones*; EFDS Publications, 1965 (WT). **Songs from Suffolk*; Bob Hart; Topic 12TS225.

Index

INDEX